50 Premium Beef Dinner Recipes for Home

By: Kelly Johnson

Table of Contents

- Beef Bourguignon
- Grilled Flank Steak with Chimichurri
- Braised Short Ribs with Red Wine
- Beef Wellington
- Classic Beef Stroganoff
- Filet Mignon with Garlic Butter
- Beef and Broccoli Stir-Fry
- Moroccan Spiced Beef Tagine
- Steak au Poivre
- Balsamic Glazed Beef Tenderloin
- Teriyaki Beef Skewers
- Beef Tacos with Chipotle Cream
- Prime Rib Roast with Horseradish Sauce
- Beef Brisket with BBQ Sauce
- Thai Basil Beef Stir-Fry
- Spicy Korean Beef Bowl
- Beef and Mushroom Risotto
- Classic Meatloaf with Glaze
- Beef Enchiladas with Green Sauce
- BBQ Beef Ribs
- Beef and Vegetable Curry
- Beef Empanadas with Chimichurri
- Herb-Crusted Roast Beef
- Peppercorn-Crusted Beef Tenderloin
- Beef Stroganoff with Egg Noodles
- Beef Fajitas with Sautéed Peppers
- Classic Cheeseburgers with Special Sauce
- Braised Beef Tacos with Pickled Onions
- Beef and Guinness Stew
- Beef Kofta Kebabs with Tzatziki

- Carne Asada with Pico de Gallo
- Beef and Bean Chili
- Stuffed Bell Peppers with Ground Beef
- Beef and Spinach Stuffed Shells
- Grilled Beef Kebabs with Vegetables
- Beef Ragu with Pappardelle
- Beef Szechuan Noodles
- Shredded Beef Tacos with Avocado
- Moroccan Beef Meatballs
- Beef Pho with Fresh Herbs
- Beef and Vegetable Stir-Fry with Rice
- Beef Bolognese with Spaghetti
- Beef Tostadas with Refried Beans
- Sweet and Sour Beef with Pineapple
- Beef Curry with Coconut Milk
- Beef Salad with Thai Dressing
- Stuffed Cabbage Rolls with Beef
- Beef and Lentil Soup
- Beef Goulash with Egg Noodles
- Beef and Cheese Quesadillas

Beef Bourguignon

Ingredients:

- 2 lbs beef chuck, cut into 1-inch cubes
- Salt and pepper to taste
- 4 oz bacon, diced
- 1 onion, chopped
- 2 carrots, sliced
- 2 cloves garlic, minced
- 2 cups red wine (Burgundy or similar)
- 2 cups beef broth
- 1 bouquet garni (thyme, bay leaf, parsley)
- 8 oz mushrooms, quartered
- 2 tbsp flour
- 2 tbsp olive oil

Instructions:

1. Preheat Oven: Preheat your oven to 325°F (163°C).
2. Brown Bacon: In a Dutch oven, cook the bacon over medium heat until crispy. Remove and set aside.
3. Sear Beef: In the bacon fat, brown the beef cubes on all sides. Remove and set aside.
4. Sauté Vegetables: In the same pot, add onion, carrots, and garlic. Sauté until softened.
5. Combine Ingredients: Return the beef and bacon to the pot. Sprinkle with flour and stir. Pour in the wine and beef broth. Add the bouquet garni.
6. Braise: Bring to a simmer, cover, and transfer to the oven. Cook for about 2.5 hours, stirring occasionally.
7. Add Mushrooms: In the last 30 minutes, add the mushrooms. Adjust seasoning if necessary.
8. Serve: Remove bouquet garni and serve with crusty bread or mashed potatoes.

Grilled Flank Steak with Chimichurri

Ingredients:

- 1 lb flank steak
- Salt and pepper to taste
- 1/2 cup chimichurri sauce (store-bought or homemade)
- Olive oil for grilling

Instructions:

1. Preheat Grill: Preheat your grill to high heat.
2. Season Steak: Rub the flank steak with olive oil, salt, and pepper.
3. Grill Steak: Grill for 5-6 minutes per side for medium-rare, or until desired doneness.
4. Rest and Slice: Let the steak rest for 5-10 minutes before slicing against the grain.
5. Serve: Drizzle with chimichurri sauce and serve.

Braised Short Ribs with Red Wine

Ingredients:

- 4 beef short ribs
- Salt and pepper to taste
- 2 tbsp olive oil
- 1 onion, chopped
- 2 carrots, chopped
- 2 cups red wine
- 1 cup beef broth
- 2 cloves garlic, minced
- 1 sprig thyme
- 1 bay leaf

Instructions:

1. Preheat Oven: Preheat your oven to 300°F (150°C).
2. Season Ribs: Season short ribs with salt and pepper.
3. Sear Ribs: Heat olive oil in a Dutch oven over medium-high heat. Sear short ribs on all sides until browned. Remove from pot.
4. Sauté Vegetables: Add onion and carrots to the pot, sautéing until softened. Add garlic and cook for another minute.
5. Braise Ribs: Return ribs to the pot. Pour in red wine and beef broth. Add thyme and bay leaf. Cover and braise in the oven for 3 hours or until tender.
6. Serve: Serve short ribs with sauce spooned over them.

Beef Wellington

Ingredients:

- 1 lb beef tenderloin
- Salt and pepper to taste
- 2 tbsp olive oil
- 8 oz mushrooms, finely chopped
- 1 tbsp Dijon mustard
- 1 sheet puff pastry
- 6 slices prosciutto
- 1 egg, beaten (for egg wash)

Instructions:

1. Preheat Oven: Preheat your oven to 400°F (200°C).
2. Sear Beef: Season beef tenderloin with salt and pepper. In a skillet, heat olive oil over high heat and sear the beef on all sides. Remove and let cool. Brush with Dijon mustard.
3. Cook Mushrooms: In the same skillet, sauté mushrooms until moisture evaporates. Let cool.
4. Wrap Beef: On a sheet of puff pastry, lay out prosciutto slices, overlapping slightly. Spread the mushrooms over the prosciutto. Place the beef on top and wrap the pastry around it, sealing the edges.
5. Bake: Place on a baking sheet, brush with egg wash, and bake for 25-30 minutes or until golden brown.
6. Serve: Let rest for 10 minutes before slicing and serving.

Classic Beef Stroganoff

Ingredients:

- 1 lb beef sirloin, cut into strips
- Salt and pepper to taste
- 2 tbsp olive oil
- 1 onion, chopped
- 2 cups mushrooms, sliced
- 2 cloves garlic, minced
- 1 cup beef broth
- 1 cup sour cream
- 2 tbsp flour
- Egg noodles for serving

Instructions:

1. Cook Noodles: Cook egg noodles according to package instructions and set aside.
2. Sear Beef: Season beef strips with salt and pepper. In a skillet, heat olive oil over medium-high heat and brown the beef in batches. Remove and set aside.
3. Sauté Vegetables: In the same skillet, add onion and mushrooms. Sauté until softened, then add garlic and cook for another minute.
4. Make Sauce: Sprinkle flour over vegetables and stir. Slowly add beef broth while stirring. Return beef to the skillet and simmer for 5 minutes.
5. Add Sour Cream: Stir in sour cream and heat through without boiling.
6. Serve: Serve the stroganoff over egg noodles.

Filet Mignon with Garlic Butter

Ingredients:

- 2 filet mignon steaks (1.5 inches thick)
- Salt and pepper to taste
- 2 tbsp olive oil
- 1/4 cup butter, softened
- 2 cloves garlic, minced
- 1 tbsp fresh parsley, chopped

Instructions:

1. Prepare Garlic Butter: In a bowl, mix softened butter with minced garlic and parsley. Set aside.
2. Season Steaks: Season the filet mignon steaks with salt and pepper.
3. Sear Steaks: Heat olive oil in a skillet over medium-high heat. Sear the steaks for 4-5 minutes per side for medium-rare.
4. Add Garlic Butter: During the last minute of cooking, add garlic butter to the pan and baste the steaks.
5. Serve: Let rest for 5 minutes and serve with additional garlic butter.

Beef and Broccoli Stir-Fry

Ingredients:

- 1 lb beef sirloin, thinly sliced
- 2 cups broccoli florets
- 2 tbsp soy sauce
- 2 tbsp oyster sauce
- 1 tbsp cornstarch
- 2 cloves garlic, minced
- 1 tbsp ginger, minced
- 2 tbsp vegetable oil
- Cooked rice for serving

Instructions:

1. Marinate Beef: In a bowl, combine beef, soy sauce, oyster sauce, and cornstarch. Let marinate for 15 minutes.
2. Blanch Broccoli: Blanch broccoli florets in boiling water for 2 minutes, then drain and set aside.
3. Stir-Fry Beef: Heat vegetable oil in a large skillet over high heat. Stir-fry the marinated beef for 2-3 minutes until browned. Remove from skillet.
4. Cook Vegetables: In the same skillet, add garlic and ginger, cooking for 30 seconds. Add blanched broccoli and stir-fry for another 2 minutes.
5. Combine and Serve: Return beef to the skillet, stir to combine, and serve over rice.

Moroccan Spiced Beef Tagine

Ingredients:

- 2 lbs beef chuck, cut into cubes
- 2 tbsp olive oil
- 1 onion, chopped
- 2 cloves garlic, minced
- 2 tsp ground cumin
- 1 tsp ground cinnamon
- 1 tsp ground ginger
- 1/2 tsp ground turmeric
- 1/2 tsp cayenne pepper (optional)
- 1 can (14 oz) diced tomatoes
- 1 cup beef broth
- 1 cup dried apricots, chopped
- 1/2 cup almonds, toasted
- Salt and pepper to taste
- Fresh cilantro for garnish

Instructions:

1. Brown Beef: In a large pot or tagine, heat olive oil over medium heat. Add beef cubes and brown on all sides. Remove and set aside.
2. Sauté Onions and Garlic: In the same pot, add onion and garlic. Sauté until softened.
3. Add Spices: Stir in cumin, cinnamon, ginger, turmeric, and cayenne pepper. Cook for 1-2 minutes until fragrant.
4. Combine Ingredients: Return beef to the pot. Add diced tomatoes, beef broth, and apricots. Season with salt and pepper.
5. Simmer: Cover and simmer for 1.5 to 2 hours until beef is tender. Stir occasionally and add water if necessary.
6. Serve: Garnish with toasted almonds and cilantro. Serve with couscous or bread.

Steak au Poivre

Ingredients:

- 2 ribeye steaks (1-inch thick)
- Salt and freshly cracked black pepper
- 2 tbsp olive oil
- 1/2 cup brandy or cognac
- 1 cup heavy cream
- 1 tbsp Dijon mustard
- 1 tbsp butter

Instructions:

1. Season Steaks: Generously season steaks with salt and cracked black pepper.
2. Sear Steaks: In a skillet, heat olive oil over medium-high heat. Add steaks and cook for 4-5 minutes per side for medium-rare. Remove and let rest.
3. Make Sauce: In the same skillet, carefully add brandy and scrape the bottom to deglaze. Allow to simmer for 2-3 minutes. Stir in cream and mustard, cooking until thickened.
4. Finish Sauce: Remove from heat and stir in butter. Adjust seasoning if needed.
5. Serve: Slice steaks and serve with the sauce drizzled over the top.

Balsamic Glazed Beef Tenderloin

Ingredients:

- 2 lbs beef tenderloin
- Salt and pepper to taste
- 2 tbsp olive oil
- 1 cup balsamic vinegar
- 1/4 cup honey
- 2 cloves garlic, minced
- 1 tsp fresh rosemary, chopped

Instructions:

1. **Preheat Oven:** Preheat oven to 400°F (200°C).
2. **Season Tenderloin:** Season the beef tenderloin with salt and pepper.
3. **Sear Beef:** In an oven-safe skillet, heat olive oil over medium-high heat. Sear the tenderloin on all sides until browned.
4. **Make Glaze:** In a bowl, mix balsamic vinegar, honey, garlic, and rosemary. Pour over the tenderloin.
5. **Bake:** Transfer the skillet to the oven and roast for 25-30 minutes, or until the internal temperature reaches desired doneness.
6. **Rest and Serve:** Let rest for 10 minutes before slicing and serving with pan juices.

Teriyaki Beef Skewers

Ingredients:

- 1 lb beef sirloin, cut into bite-sized pieces
- 1/2 cup teriyaki sauce
- 2 tbsp sesame oil
- 2 green onions, chopped
- 1 bell pepper, cut into chunks
- Wooden skewers (soaked in water)

Instructions:

1. Marinate Beef: In a bowl, combine beef, teriyaki sauce, and sesame oil. Let marinate for at least 30 minutes.
2. Prepare Skewers: Thread marinated beef, green onions, and bell pepper onto skewers.
3. Preheat Grill: Preheat the grill to medium-high heat.
4. Grill Skewers: Grill skewers for 8-10 minutes, turning occasionally until beef is cooked through.
5. Serve: Serve hot with additional teriyaki sauce for dipping.

Beef Tacos with Chipotle Cream

Ingredients:

- 1 lb ground beef
- 1 packet taco seasoning
- 12 taco shells
- 1 cup lettuce, shredded
- 1 cup tomato, diced
- 1/2 cup cheese, shredded
- 1/2 cup sour cream
- 1-2 chipotle peppers in adobo sauce, minced

Instructions:

1. Cook Beef: In a skillet over medium heat, cook ground beef until browned. Drain excess fat and add taco seasoning. Follow package instructions.
2. Make Chipotle Cream: In a small bowl, mix sour cream with minced chipotle peppers.
3. Assemble Tacos: Fill taco shells with seasoned beef and top with lettuce, tomatoes, cheese, and chipotle cream.
4. Serve: Serve immediately with lime wedges.

Prime Rib Roast with Horseradish Sauce

Ingredients:

- 5-6 lbs prime rib roast
- Salt and pepper to taste
- 2 tbsp olive oil
- 2 cloves garlic, minced
- 1/4 cup horseradish sauce
- 1/4 cup sour cream
- 1 tbsp Dijon mustard

Instructions:

1. Preheat Oven: Preheat your oven to 450°F (230°C).
2. Season Roast: Rub the roast with olive oil, garlic, salt, and pepper.
3. Roast: Place the prime rib in a roasting pan and roast for 20 minutes. Reduce temperature to 325°F (163°C) and roast for an additional 1.5-2 hours, or until the desired internal temperature is reached.
4. Make Sauce: In a bowl, mix horseradish sauce, sour cream, and Dijon mustard.
5. Serve: Let the roast rest for 15-20 minutes before slicing. Serve with horseradish sauce on the side.

Beef Brisket with BBQ Sauce

Ingredients:

- 3-4 lbs beef brisket
- Salt and pepper to taste
- 2 tbsp olive oil
- 2 cups BBQ sauce (store-bought or homemade)
- 1 onion, sliced
- 2 cloves garlic, minced

Instructions:

1. **Preheat Oven:** Preheat your oven to 300°F (150°C).
2. **Season Brisket:** Season brisket with salt and pepper.
3. **Sear Brisket:** In a large oven-safe pot, heat olive oil over medium-high heat. Sear the brisket on all sides until browned. Remove and set aside.
4. **Sauté Vegetables:** In the same pot, add onion and garlic, sautéing until softened.
5. **Braise Brisket:** Return brisket to the pot, add BBQ sauce, and cover. Cook in the oven for 3-4 hours, or until tender.
6. **Serve:** Let rest for 15 minutes before slicing. Serve with additional BBQ sauce.

Thai Basil Beef Stir-Fry

Ingredients:

- 1 lb ground beef
- 1 cup fresh basil leaves (Thai basil preferred)
- 3 cloves garlic, minced
- 1-2 Thai chilies, chopped (adjust to taste)
- 2 tbsp soy sauce
- 1 tbsp oyster sauce
- 1 tbsp fish sauce
- 1 tbsp sugar
- 1 tbsp vegetable oil
- Cooked rice for serving

Instructions:

1. Heat Oil: In a large skillet or wok, heat the vegetable oil over medium-high heat.
2. Cook Beef: Add ground beef, breaking it apart as it cooks until browned.
3. Add Aromatics: Stir in garlic and Thai chilies. Cook for 1-2 minutes until fragrant.
4. Add Sauces: Mix in soy sauce, oyster sauce, fish sauce, and sugar. Stir well to combine.
5. Add Basil: Remove from heat and fold in the basil leaves until wilted.
6. Serve: Serve hot over cooked rice.

Spicy Korean Beef Bowl

Ingredients:

- 1 lb flank steak, thinly sliced
- 2 tbsp soy sauce
- 1 tbsp gochujang (Korean chili paste)
- 1 tbsp sesame oil
- 2 cloves garlic, minced
- 1 inch ginger, grated
- 1 cup cooked rice
- 1 cup vegetables (carrots, bell peppers, broccoli)
- Sesame seeds for garnish
- Green onions for garnish

Instructions:

1. Marinate Beef: In a bowl, combine soy sauce, gochujang, sesame oil, garlic, and ginger. Add sliced beef and marinate for at least 30 minutes.
2. Cook Vegetables: In a pan, stir-fry vegetables until tender. Remove and set aside.
3. Cook Beef: In the same pan, stir-fry the marinated beef until cooked through.
4. Assemble Bowls: Divide rice among bowls, top with beef and vegetables.
5. Garnish: Sprinkle with sesame seeds and green onions. Serve hot.

Beef and Mushroom Risotto

Ingredients:

- 1 lb ground beef
- 1 cup Arborio rice
- 4 cups beef broth
- 1 cup mushrooms, sliced
- 1 onion, chopped
- 2 cloves garlic, minced
- 1/2 cup white wine (optional)
- 1/2 cup Parmesan cheese, grated
- 2 tbsp olive oil
- Salt and pepper to taste
- Fresh parsley for garnish

Instructions:

1. Sauté Vegetables: In a pot, heat olive oil over medium heat. Add onion and garlic, cooking until soft.
2. Add Mushrooms: Stir in mushrooms and cook until browned.
3. Add Beef: Add ground beef, cooking until browned. Drain excess fat.
4. Cook Rice: Add Arborio rice, stirring for 1-2 minutes. Pour in wine, stirring until absorbed.
5. Add Broth: Gradually add beef broth, one ladle at a time, stirring until absorbed before adding more.
6. Finish Risotto: Once rice is creamy and al dente, stir in Parmesan cheese. Season with salt and pepper. Garnish with parsley.

Classic Meatloaf with Glaze

Ingredients:

- 1 lb ground beef
- 1/2 cup breadcrumbs
- 1/2 cup onion, finely chopped
- 1/4 cup milk
- 1 egg
- 2 tbsp Worcestershire sauce
- Salt and pepper to taste
- 1/2 cup ketchup (for glaze)

Instructions:

1. Preheat Oven: Preheat oven to 350°F (175°C).
2. Mix Ingredients: In a large bowl, combine ground beef, breadcrumbs, onion, milk, egg, Worcestershire sauce, salt, and pepper. Mix well.
3. Form Loaf: Shape mixture into a loaf and place in a baking dish.
4. Add Glaze: Spread ketchup evenly over the top of the meatloaf.
5. Bake: Bake for 1 hour, or until the internal temperature reaches 160°F (70°C).
6. Serve: Let rest for a few minutes before slicing and serving.

Beef Enchiladas with Green Sauce

Ingredients:

- 1 lb ground beef
- 1 cup shredded cheese (cheddar or Mexican blend)
- 8 corn tortillas
- 1 can (10 oz) green enchilada sauce
- 1/2 cup onion, chopped
- 1 tsp cumin
- Salt and pepper to taste
- Fresh cilantro for garnish

Instructions:

1. Cook Beef: In a skillet, cook ground beef and onion until browned. Season with cumin, salt, and pepper.
2. Preheat Oven: Preheat oven to 350°F (175°C).
3. Prepare Tortillas: Warm tortillas in a skillet or microwave to soften.
4. Fill Tortillas: Place beef mixture in each tortilla, roll up, and place seam-side down in a baking dish.
5. Add Sauce: Pour green enchilada sauce over the enchiladas and sprinkle with cheese.
6. Bake: Bake for 20-25 minutes until cheese is melted and bubbly. Garnish with cilantro.

BBQ Beef Ribs

Ingredients:

- 3-4 lbs beef ribs
- 1 cup BBQ sauce (store-bought or homemade)
- Salt and pepper to taste
- 1 tbsp garlic powder
- 1 tbsp onion powder
- 1 tbsp smoked paprika

Instructions:

1. Preheat Oven: Preheat oven to 300°F (150°C).
2. Season Ribs: Rub ribs with salt, pepper, garlic powder, onion powder, and smoked paprika.
3. Wrap in Foil: Wrap ribs tightly in aluminum foil and place on a baking sheet.
4. Bake: Bake for 3 hours, until tender.
5. Add Sauce: Remove from foil, brush with BBQ sauce, and return to oven uncovered for 30 minutes.
6. Serve: Serve hot with additional BBQ sauce on the side.

Beef and Vegetable Curry

Ingredients:

- 1 lb beef (chuck or sirloin), cut into cubes
- 1 onion, chopped
- 2 cloves garlic, minced
- 1 inch ginger, grated
- 2 cups mixed vegetables (carrots, bell peppers, peas)
- 1 can (14 oz) coconut milk
- 2 tbsp curry powder
- 2 tbsp vegetable oil
- Salt to taste
- Fresh cilantro for garnish

Instructions:

1. Sauté Aromatics: In a large pot, heat oil over medium heat. Add onion, garlic, and ginger. Cook until softened.
2. Brown Beef: Add beef cubes and brown on all sides.
3. Add Spices: Stir in curry powder and cook for 1 minute.
4. Add Coconut Milk: Pour in coconut milk and bring to a simmer. Cook for 1 hour until beef is tender.
5. Add Vegetables: Stir in mixed vegetables and cook for an additional 15-20 minutes until tender.
6. Serve: Garnish with cilantro and serve hot with rice or naan.

Beef Empanadas with Chimichurri

Ingredients:

For the Empanada Dough:

- 2 cups all-purpose flour
- 1/2 cup unsalted butter, chilled and cubed
- 1/2 tsp salt
- 1/4 cup cold water

For the Filling:

- 1 lb ground beef
- 1 onion, finely chopped
- 2 cloves garlic, minced
- 1 tsp cumin
- 1 tsp paprika
- Salt and pepper to taste

For the Chimichurri:

- 1 cup fresh parsley
- 1/2 cup olive oil
- 1/4 cup red wine vinegar
- 2 cloves garlic
- 1 tsp oregano
- Salt and pepper to taste

Instructions:

1. Make the Dough: In a bowl, mix flour and salt. Cut in butter until the mixture resembles coarse crumbs. Stir in cold water until the dough comes together. Wrap in plastic and chill for 30 minutes.
2. Prepare the Filling: In a skillet, cook onion and garlic until soft. Add ground beef, cumin, paprika, salt, and pepper. Cook until browned. Let cool.
3. Make Chimichurri: Blend all chimichurri ingredients until smooth. Adjust seasoning.
4. Assemble Empanadas: Roll out dough and cut into circles. Place filling in the center, fold, and crimp edges to seal.

5. Bake: Preheat oven to 375°F (190°C). Place empanadas on a baking sheet and bake for 25-30 minutes until golden brown.
6. Serve: Serve warm with chimichurri sauce.

Herb-Crusted Roast Beef

Ingredients:

- 3-4 lb beef roast (sirloin or ribeye)
- 2 tbsp olive oil
- 3 cloves garlic, minced
- 1 tbsp fresh rosemary, chopped
- 1 tbsp fresh thyme, chopped
- 1 tbsp Dijon mustard
- Salt and pepper to taste

Instructions:

1. Preheat Oven: Preheat oven to 375°F (190°C).
2. Prepare Roast: In a bowl, mix olive oil, garlic, rosemary, thyme, mustard, salt, and pepper. Rub mixture all over the beef roast.
3. Roast Beef: Place the roast in a roasting pan and cook for 1.5-2 hours or until the internal temperature reaches your desired doneness.
4. Rest: Remove from oven and let rest for 15-20 minutes before slicing.
5. Serve: Serve with your choice of sides.

Peppercorn-Crusted Beef Tenderloin

Ingredients:

- 2 lb beef tenderloin
- 2 tbsp whole black peppercorns
- 2 tbsp olive oil
- 1 tbsp Dijon mustard
- Salt to taste

Instructions:

1. Preheat Oven: Preheat oven to 400°F (200°C).
2. Crust the Beef: Crush peppercorns and mix with salt. Rub the beef with olive oil and mustard, then coat with pepper mixture.
3. Sear the Tenderloin: In a skillet, sear the tenderloin on all sides over high heat.
4. Roast: Transfer to the oven and roast for 20-25 minutes for medium-rare. Use a meat thermometer to check doneness.
5. Rest: Let rest for 10 minutes before slicing.
6. Serve: Serve with your favorite sauce or sides.

Beef Stroganoff with Egg Noodles

Ingredients:

- 1 lb beef sirloin, thinly sliced
- 8 oz egg noodles
- 1 cup mushrooms, sliced
- 1 onion, chopped
- 2 cloves garlic, minced
- 1 cup beef broth
- 1 cup sour cream
- 2 tbsp flour
- 2 tbsp olive oil
- Salt and pepper to taste

Instructions:

1. Cook Noodles: Cook egg noodles according to package instructions. Drain and set aside.
2. Sauté Beef: In a skillet, heat olive oil and sauté beef until browned. Remove from pan.
3. Cook Vegetables: In the same skillet, add onion, garlic, and mushrooms. Cook until soft.
4. Make Sauce: Sprinkle flour over the vegetables, stir to combine, then slowly add beef broth. Bring to a simmer and stir until thickened.
5. Add Beef and Sour Cream: Return beef to the skillet and stir in sour cream. Cook until heated through. Season with salt and pepper.
6. Serve: Serve over egg noodles.

Beef Fajitas with Sautéed Peppers

Ingredients:

- 1 lb flank steak
- 1 bell pepper (any color), sliced
- 1 onion, sliced
- 2 tbsp olive oil
- 2 tsp fajita seasoning
- Salt and pepper to taste
- Tortillas for serving

Instructions:

1. Marinate Steak: Rub flank steak with olive oil, fajita seasoning, salt, and pepper. Let marinate for 30 minutes.
2. Cook Steak: Heat a skillet over high heat. Cook the steak for about 5-7 minutes on each side for medium-rare. Remove and let rest.
3. Sauté Peppers: In the same skillet, add more olive oil if needed and sauté peppers and onion until tender.
4. Slice Steak: Slice the steak against the grain.
5. Serve: Serve steak with sautéed peppers in warm tortillas.

Classic Cheeseburgers with Special Sauce

Ingredients:

- 1 lb ground beef
- 4 burger buns
- 4 slices cheddar cheese
- 1/4 cup mayonnaise
- 2 tbsp ketchup
- 1 tbsp mustard
- 1 tbsp pickles, chopped
- Salt and pepper to taste

Instructions:

1. **Make Special Sauce:** In a bowl, mix mayonnaise, ketchup, mustard, and pickles. Set aside.
2. **Form Patties:** Shape ground beef into four patties. Season with salt and pepper.
3. **Cook Patties:** Heat a grill or skillet over medium-high heat. Cook patties for about 4-5 minutes on each side. Add cheese during the last minute of cooking to melt.
4. **Toast Buns:** Lightly toast burger buns on the grill.
5. **Assemble Burgers:** Spread special sauce on the buns, add the cheeseburger patty, and top with your favorite toppings (lettuce, tomato, onion).
6. **Serve:** Serve immediately.

Braised Beef Tacos with Pickled Onions

Ingredients:

- 2 lb beef chuck roast
- 1 onion, chopped
- 2 cloves garlic, minced
- 1 can (14 oz) diced tomatoes
- 2 cups beef broth
- 1 tbsp chili powder
- 1 tsp cumin
- Salt and pepper to taste
- Corn tortillas for serving

For the Pickled Onions:

- 1 onion, thinly sliced
- 1/2 cup vinegar (white or apple cider)
- 1/2 cup water
- 1 tbsp sugar
- Salt to taste

Instructions:

1. Make Pickled Onions: In a saucepan, combine vinegar, water, sugar, and salt. Bring to a boil, then pour over sliced onions in a jar. Let cool and refrigerate.
2. Brown the Beef: In a pot, brown the beef on all sides. Remove and set aside.
3. Sauté Aromatics: In the same pot, cook onion and garlic until soft. Add diced tomatoes, beef broth, chili powder, cumin, salt, and pepper.
4. Braise Beef: Return beef to the pot. Cover and simmer for 2-3 hours until tender.
5. Shred Beef: Shred the beef with two forks.
6. Serve: Serve shredded beef in corn tortillas, topped with pickled onions.

Beef and Guinness Stew

Ingredients:

- 2 lbs beef chuck, cut into 1-inch cubes
- 3 tbsp olive oil
- 1 onion, chopped
- 2 carrots, sliced
- 2 cloves garlic, minced
- 2 tbsp tomato paste
- 1 bottle (12 oz) Guinness stout
- 4 cups beef broth
- 1 tsp thyme
- 1 bay leaf
- Salt and pepper to taste
- 2 cups potatoes, diced

Instructions:

1. Brown the Beef: In a large pot, heat olive oil over medium-high heat. Season beef with salt and pepper, then brown in batches. Remove and set aside.
2. Sauté Vegetables: In the same pot, add onions, carrots, and garlic. Cook until softened, about 5 minutes. Stir in tomato paste and cook for another minute.
3. Add Liquid: Return the beef to the pot. Pour in the Guinness and beef broth. Add thyme, bay leaf, and bring to a boil.
4. Simmer: Reduce heat to low, cover, and simmer for 1.5 to 2 hours. Add potatoes halfway through cooking.
5. Serve: Remove bay leaf and adjust seasoning. Serve hot with crusty bread.

Beef Kofta Kebabs with Tzatziki

Ingredients:

For the Kofta:

- 1 lb ground beef
- 1 small onion, grated
- 2 cloves garlic, minced
- 1 tsp cumin
- 1 tsp coriander
- 1 tsp paprika
- Salt and pepper to taste

For the Tzatziki:

- 1 cup Greek yogurt
- 1 cucumber, grated and drained
- 2 cloves garlic, minced
- 1 tbsp olive oil
- 1 tbsp vinegar
- Salt and pepper to taste

Instructions:

1. Make Kofta Mixture: In a bowl, combine ground beef, onion, garlic, spices, salt, and pepper. Mix well and shape into long kebabs on skewers.
2. Grill Koftas: Preheat grill to medium-high heat. Grill koftas for about 10-12 minutes, turning occasionally.
3. Make Tzatziki: In another bowl, mix yogurt, cucumber, garlic, olive oil, vinegar, salt, and pepper.
4. Serve: Serve koftas with tzatziki sauce and pita bread or rice.

Carne Asada with Pico de Gallo

Ingredients:

For the Carne Asada:

- 1.5 lbs flank steak
- 2 tbsp olive oil
- 2 tbsp lime juice
- 2 cloves garlic, minced
- 1 tsp cumin
- 1 tsp chili powder
- Salt and pepper to taste

For the Pico de Gallo:

- 2 tomatoes, diced
- 1 onion, diced
- 1 jalapeño, minced
- 1/4 cup cilantro, chopped
- 1 tbsp lime juice
- Salt to taste

Instructions:

1. Marinate Steak: Combine olive oil, lime juice, garlic, cumin, chili powder, salt, and pepper in a bowl. Add steak and marinate for at least 1 hour.
2. Make Pico de Gallo: Mix all pico de gallo ingredients in a bowl. Set aside.
3. Grill Steak: Preheat grill to high heat. Grill steak for 5-7 minutes on each side for medium-rare. Let rest before slicing.
4. Serve: Serve sliced steak with pico de gallo and tortillas.

Beef and Bean Chili

Ingredients:

- 1 lb ground beef
- 1 onion, chopped
- 2 cloves garlic, minced
- 1 can (14 oz) diced tomatoes
- 1 can (15 oz) kidney beans, drained
- 1 can (15 oz) black beans, drained
- 2 tbsp chili powder
- 1 tsp cumin
- Salt and pepper to taste

Instructions:

1. Brown Beef: In a large pot, brown ground beef over medium heat. Drain excess fat.
2. Sauté Vegetables: Add onion and garlic. Cook until softened.
3. Add Remaining Ingredients: Stir in tomatoes, beans, chili powder, cumin, salt, and pepper. Bring to a boil.
4. Simmer: Reduce heat and simmer for 20-30 minutes.
5. Serve: Serve hot with cornbread or rice.

Stuffed Bell Peppers with Ground Beef

Ingredients:

- 4 bell peppers (any color)
- 1 lb ground beef
- 1 cup cooked rice
- 1 onion, chopped
- 1 can (14 oz) diced tomatoes
- 1 tsp Italian seasoning
- Salt and pepper to taste
- 1 cup shredded cheese (optional)

Instructions:

1. Preheat Oven: Preheat oven to 375°F (190°C).
2. Prepare Peppers: Cut the tops off the bell peppers and remove seeds.
3. Make Filling: In a skillet, cook onion until soft. Add ground beef and cook until browned. Stir in rice, tomatoes, Italian seasoning, salt, and pepper.
4. Stuff Peppers: Fill each pepper with the beef mixture. Place in a baking dish. If using, top with cheese.
5. Bake: Cover with foil and bake for 30 minutes. Remove foil and bake for an additional 10-15 minutes.
6. Serve: Serve hot.

Beef and Spinach Stuffed Shells

Ingredients:

- 12 jumbo pasta shells
- 1 lb ground beef
- 1 cup spinach, chopped
- 1 cup ricotta cheese
- 1 cup marinara sauce
- 1 cup shredded mozzarella cheese
- 1/2 cup Parmesan cheese
- Salt and pepper to taste

Instructions:

1. Preheat Oven: Preheat oven to 375°F (190°C).
2. Cook Shells: Cook pasta shells according to package instructions. Drain and set aside.
3. Make Filling: In a skillet, cook ground beef until browned. Stir in spinach, ricotta, salt, and pepper.
4. Stuff Shells: Fill each shell with the beef and spinach mixture. Place in a baking dish. Top with marinara sauce and mozzarella cheese.
5. Bake: Bake for 25-30 minutes until heated through and cheese is melted.
6. Serve: Serve hot, garnished with Parmesan cheese.

Grilled Beef Kebabs with Vegetables

Ingredients:

- 1 lb beef sirloin, cubed
- 1 bell pepper, cubed
- 1 onion, cubed
- 1 zucchini, sliced
- 2 tbsp olive oil
- 2 tbsp soy sauce
- 1 tsp garlic powder
- Salt and pepper to taste

Instructions:

1. Marinate Beef: In a bowl, mix olive oil, soy sauce, garlic powder, salt, and pepper. Add cubed beef and marinate for at least 30 minutes.
2. Prepare Skewers: Thread beef and vegetables onto skewers.
3. Grill Kebabs: Preheat grill to medium-high heat. Grill kebabs for about 10-12 minutes, turning occasionally until beef is cooked to desired doneness.
4. Serve: Serve hot with rice or a salad.

Beef Ragu with Pappardelle

Ingredients:

- 2 lbs beef chuck, cut into 1-inch pieces
- 2 tbsp olive oil
- 1 onion, chopped
- 2 carrots, diced
- 2 celery stalks, diced
- 3 cloves garlic, minced
- 1 cup red wine
- 1 can (28 oz) crushed tomatoes
- 2 cups beef broth
- 1 tsp dried oregano
- Salt and pepper to taste
- 12 oz pappardelle pasta
- Grated Parmesan cheese for serving

Instructions:

1. Brown the Beef: In a large pot, heat olive oil over medium-high heat. Season beef with salt and pepper, then brown in batches. Remove and set aside.
2. Sauté Vegetables: In the same pot, add onion, carrots, and celery. Cook until softened, about 5-7 minutes. Stir in garlic and cook for an additional minute.
3. Add Liquid: Pour in red wine, scraping the bottom of the pot. Add crushed tomatoes, beef broth, oregano, and the browned beef. Bring to a boil.
4. Simmer: Reduce heat to low, cover, and simmer for about 2-3 hours, stirring occasionally until the beef is tender.
5. Cook Pasta: Cook pappardelle according to package instructions. Drain and toss with the ragu.
6. Serve: Serve hot, garnished with grated Parmesan cheese.

Beef Szechuan Noodles

Ingredients:

- 1 lb beef flank steak, thinly sliced
- 2 tbsp soy sauce
- 2 tbsp cornstarch
- 2 tbsp vegetable oil
- 1 bell pepper, sliced
- 1 cup snap peas
- 2 cloves garlic, minced
- 1 tbsp ginger, minced
- 1/4 cup Szechuan sauce
- 8 oz noodles (e.g., egg noodles or rice noodles)
- Green onions for garnish

Instructions:

1. Marinate Beef: In a bowl, combine beef, soy sauce, and cornstarch. Let sit for 15 minutes.
2. Cook Noodles: Cook noodles according to package instructions, drain, and set aside.
3. Stir-Fry Beef: In a large skillet or wok, heat oil over medium-high heat. Stir-fry beef until browned, about 3-4 minutes. Remove and set aside.
4. Stir-Fry Vegetables: In the same pan, add bell pepper and snap peas. Stir-fry for 2-3 minutes, then add garlic and ginger. Cook for another minute.
5. Combine: Add the beef back to the pan, along with Szechuan sauce and cooked noodles. Toss to combine and heat through.
6. Serve: Serve hot, garnished with green onions.

Shredded Beef Tacos with Avocado

Ingredients:

- 2 lbs beef chuck roast
- 1 onion, quartered
- 2 cloves garlic, minced
- 1 cup beef broth
- 1 tbsp cumin
- 1 tbsp chili powder
- Salt and pepper to taste
- Corn tortillas
- 1 avocado, sliced
- Fresh cilantro for garnish

Instructions:

1. Cook Beef: In a slow cooker, combine beef, onion, garlic, beef broth, cumin, chili powder, salt, and pepper. Cook on low for 8 hours or until beef is tender.
2. Shred Beef: Remove the beef from the slow cooker and shred with two forks.
3. Warm Tortillas: Warm corn tortillas in a skillet or microwave.
4. Assemble Tacos: Fill each tortilla with shredded beef and top with avocado slices and cilantro.
5. Serve: Serve immediately with lime wedges on the side.

Moroccan Beef Meatballs

Ingredients:

- 1 lb ground beef
- 1/2 cup breadcrumbs
- 1/4 cup parsley, chopped
- 2 cloves garlic, minced
- 1 tsp cumin
- 1 tsp coriander
- 1 tsp paprika
- 1/2 tsp cinnamon
- Salt and pepper to taste
- 1 can (15 oz) diced tomatoes
- 1 cup beef broth
- Cooked couscous for serving

Instructions:

1. Make Meatballs: In a bowl, combine ground beef, breadcrumbs, parsley, garlic, spices, salt, and pepper. Form into small meatballs.
2. Brown Meatballs: In a skillet, heat olive oil over medium heat. Add meatballs and cook until browned on all sides. Remove and set aside.
3. Simmer Sauce: In the same skillet, add diced tomatoes and beef broth. Bring to a simmer.
4. Cook Meatballs: Return meatballs to the skillet. Cover and simmer for 20 minutes.
5. Serve: Serve meatballs over cooked couscous.

Beef Pho with Fresh Herbs

Ingredients:

- 1 lb beef sirloin, thinly sliced
- 8 cups beef broth
- 1 onion, quartered
- 1 piece ginger, sliced
- 2 star anise
- 1 cinnamon stick
- Rice noodles
- Fresh herbs (basil, cilantro, mint)
- Bean sprouts, lime wedges, and jalapeños for serving

Instructions:

1. Prepare Broth: In a pot, combine beef broth, onion, ginger, star anise, and cinnamon stick. Bring to a simmer and cook for 30 minutes.
2. Cook Noodles: Cook rice noodles according to package instructions, drain, and set aside.
3. Assemble Bowls: In serving bowls, place cooked noodles and top with raw beef slices. Pour hot broth over the beef to cook it.
4. Serve: Serve with fresh herbs, bean sprouts, lime wedges, and jalapeños.

Beef and Vegetable Stir-Fry with Rice

Ingredients:

- 1 lb beef sirloin, thinly sliced
- 2 tbsp soy sauce
- 2 tbsp oyster sauce
- 1 tbsp cornstarch
- 2 tbsp vegetable oil
- 1 bell pepper, sliced
- 1 carrot, julienned
- 1 cup broccoli florets
- 2 cloves garlic, minced
- Cooked rice for serving

Instructions:

1. Marinate Beef: In a bowl, mix beef with soy sauce, oyster sauce, and cornstarch. Let marinate for 15 minutes.
2. Stir-Fry Beef: In a large skillet or wok, heat oil over medium-high heat. Stir-fry beef until browned. Remove and set aside.
3. Stir-Fry Vegetables: In the same pan, add bell pepper, carrot, and broccoli. Stir-fry for 3-4 minutes, then add garlic and cook for another minute.
4. Combine: Return beef to the pan and toss to combine. Heat through.
5. Serve: Serve hot over cooked rice.

Beef Bolognese with Spaghetti

Ingredients:

- 1 lb ground beef
- 1 onion, chopped
- 2 carrots, diced
- 2 celery stalks, diced
- 2 cloves garlic, minced
- 1 cup red wine
- 1 can (28 oz) crushed tomatoes
- 1 tsp dried oregano
- Salt and pepper to taste
- 12 oz spaghetti
- Grated Parmesan cheese for serving

Instructions:

1. Brown Beef: In a large pot, cook ground beef over medium heat until browned. Drain excess fat.
2. Sauté Vegetables: Add onion, carrots, celery, and garlic. Cook until softened, about 5-7 minutes.
3. Add Liquid: Pour in red wine, scraping the bottom of the pot. Stir in crushed tomatoes, oregano, salt, and pepper. Simmer for about 30 minutes.
4. Cook Pasta: Cook spaghetti according to package instructions. Drain and toss with Bolognese sauce.
5. Serve: Serve hot, garnished with grated Parmesan cheese.

Beef Tostadas with Refried Beans

Ingredients:

- 8 tostada shells
- 2 cups refried beans
- 1 lb ground beef
- 1 tsp chili powder
- 1 tsp cumin
- Salt and pepper to taste
- 1 cup shredded lettuce
- 1 cup diced tomatoes
- 1 cup shredded cheese (cheddar or Mexican blend)
- Sour cream and salsa for serving

Instructions:

1. Cook Beef: In a skillet over medium heat, brown the ground beef. Add chili powder, cumin, salt, and pepper. Stir until well combined, and cook for 5-7 minutes.
2. Warm Beans: In a small saucepan, heat the refried beans until warm.
3. Assemble Tostadas: Spread a layer of refried beans on each tostada shell. Top with seasoned beef, shredded lettuce, diced tomatoes, and cheese.
4. Serve: Serve with sour cream and salsa on the side.

Sweet and Sour Beef with Pineapple

Ingredients:

- 1 lb beef sirloin, cut into thin strips
- 1 cup pineapple chunks (fresh or canned)
- 1 bell pepper, sliced
- 1 onion, sliced
- 2 cloves garlic, minced
- 1/4 cup soy sauce
- 1/4 cup vinegar
- 1/4 cup brown sugar
- 2 tbsp cornstarch mixed with 2 tbsp water
- Cooked rice for serving

Instructions:

1. Prepare Sauce: In a bowl, mix soy sauce, vinegar, and brown sugar. Set aside.
2. Cook Beef: In a large skillet, cook beef strips over medium-high heat until browned. Remove and set aside.
3. Sauté Vegetables: In the same skillet, add onion, bell pepper, and garlic. Cook until vegetables are tender.
4. Combine: Return beef to the skillet. Add pineapple chunks and sweet and sour sauce. Bring to a simmer.
5. Thicken Sauce: Stir in the cornstarch mixture and cook until sauce thickens.
6. Serve: Serve hot over cooked rice.

Beef Curry with Coconut Milk

Ingredients:

- 1 lb beef stew meat, cut into cubes
- 2 tbsp curry powder
- 1 can (14 oz) coconut milk
- 1 onion, chopped
- 2 cloves garlic, minced
- 1-inch piece ginger, grated
- 2 cups beef broth
- 2 carrots, sliced
- Salt and pepper to taste
- Cooked rice for serving

Instructions:

1. Brown Beef: In a pot, brown the beef cubes over medium heat. Remove and set aside.
2. Sauté Aromatics: In the same pot, add onion, garlic, and ginger. Sauté until onion is translucent.
3. Add Ingredients: Return beef to the pot. Stir in curry powder, coconut milk, beef broth, and carrots. Bring to a boil.
4. Simmer: Reduce heat, cover, and simmer for about 1-1.5 hours until the beef is tender. Season with salt and pepper.
5. Serve: Serve hot over cooked rice.

Beef Salad with Thai Dressing

Ingredients:

- 1 lb beef flank steak, grilled and sliced
- 4 cups mixed salad greens
- 1 cup cherry tomatoes, halved
- 1 cucumber, sliced
- 1/4 cup red onion, thinly sliced
- 1/4 cup fresh cilantro
- For the Dressing:
    - 2 tbsp fish sauce
    - 2 tbsp lime juice
    - 1 tbsp sugar
    - 1 clove garlic, minced
    - 1 chili pepper, sliced (optional)

Instructions:

1. Grill Beef: Grill the flank steak to desired doneness. Allow it to rest before slicing.
2. Prepare Dressing: In a bowl, whisk together fish sauce, lime juice, sugar, garlic, and chili pepper.
3. Assemble Salad: In a large bowl, combine salad greens, cherry tomatoes, cucumber, red onion, and sliced beef.
4. Dress Salad: Drizzle with the Thai dressing and toss to combine.
5. Serve: Serve immediately, garnished with fresh cilantro.

Stuffed Cabbage Rolls with Beef

Ingredients:

- 1 large head of cabbage
- 1 lb ground beef
- 1 cup cooked rice
- 1 onion, chopped
- 2 cloves garlic, minced
- 1 can (15 oz) tomato sauce
- 1 tsp paprika
- Salt and pepper to taste
- 1 cup beef broth

Instructions:

1. Prepare Cabbage: Boil the cabbage head in water until leaves are tender. Carefully peel off the leaves.
2. Make Filling: In a bowl, combine ground beef, cooked rice, onion, garlic, paprika, salt, and pepper.
3. Stuff Rolls: Place a spoonful of filling on each cabbage leaf and roll tightly, tucking in the sides.
4. Cook Rolls: In a large pot, layer some tomato sauce on the bottom. Place cabbage rolls seam-side down. Pour remaining tomato sauce and beef broth over the rolls. Cover and simmer for about 1 hour.
5. Serve: Serve hot, spooning sauce over the rolls.

Beef and Lentil Soup

Ingredients:

- 1 lb ground beef
- 1 cup lentils, rinsed
- 1 onion, chopped
- 2 carrots, diced
- 2 celery stalks, diced
- 2 cloves garlic, minced
- 6 cups beef broth
- 1 tsp thyme
- Salt and pepper to taste

Instructions:

1. Brown Beef: In a large pot, brown the ground beef over medium heat. Drain excess fat.
2. Sauté Vegetables: Add onion, carrots, celery, and garlic. Cook until vegetables are tender.
3. Add Ingredients: Stir in lentils, beef broth, thyme, salt, and pepper. Bring to a boil.
4. Simmer: Reduce heat and simmer for about 30-40 minutes, or until lentils are tender.
5. Serve: Serve hot, garnished with fresh herbs if desired.

Beef Goulash with Egg Noodles

Ingredients:

- 1 lb beef chuck, cut into cubes
- 1 onion, chopped
- 2 cloves garlic, minced
- 1 bell pepper, diced
- 2 cups beef broth
- 2 tbsp paprika
- Salt and pepper to taste
- 8 oz egg noodles
- Sour cream for serving (optional)

Instructions:

1. Brown Beef: In a large pot, brown beef cubes over medium heat. Remove and set aside.
2. Sauté Vegetables: In the same pot, add onion, garlic, and bell pepper. Cook until softened.
3. Combine: Return beef to the pot. Stir in beef broth, paprika, salt, and pepper. Bring to a simmer.
4. Cook Goulash: Cover and simmer for about 1-1.5 hours until beef is tender.
5. Cook Noodles: In a separate pot, cook egg noodles according to package instructions. Drain and add to the goulash.
6. Serve: Serve hot, garnished with sour cream if desired.

Beef and Cheese Quesadillas

Ingredients:

- 1 lb ground beef
- 1 onion, chopped
- 2 cups shredded cheese (cheddar or Mexican blend)
- 8 flour tortillas
- 1 tsp taco seasoning
- Sour cream and salsa for serving

Instructions:

1. Cook Beef: In a skillet over medium heat, cook ground beef and onion until browned. Stir in taco seasoning and cook for an additional minute.
2. Assemble Quesadillas: On half of each tortilla, spread a layer of beef mixture and top with cheese. Fold the other half over.
3. Cook Quesadillas: In the same skillet, cook quesadillas for 2-3 minutes on each side until golden and cheese is melted.
4. Serve: Cut into wedges and serve hot with sour cream and salsa.